The *Incredible* Hunt *for the* Giant Squid

Brad Matsen

Enslow Publishers, Inc.

40 Industrial Road   PO Box 38
Box 398   Aldershot
Berkeley Heights, NJ 07922   Hants GU12 6BP
USA   UK

http://www.enslow.com

Library of Congress Cataloging-in-Publication Data

Matsen, Bradford.
   The incredible hunt for the giant squid / Brad Matsen.
     p. cm. — (Incredible deep-sea adventures)
   Summary: Relates what is known about one of the largest and most mysterious
creatures of the sea, the giant squid, and what scientists are doing to learn more
about it.
   Includes bibliographical references (p.   ) and index.
   ISBN 0-7660-2192-0 (hardcover)
   1. Giant squids—Juvenile literature. [1. Giant squids. 2. Squids.] I. Title.
II. Series: Matsen, Bradford. Incredible deep-sea adventures.
   QL430.3.A73 M38 2003
   594'.58—dc21
                                 2002153921

Printed in the United States of America

10 9 8 7 6 5 4 3 2 1

Contents

CHAPTER 1

Battle of *the* Giants

his story begins with a sperm whale. He is cruising in the Pacific Ocean looking for food. He is sixty feet (eighteen meters) long. He weighs 120,000 pounds (54,000 kilograms), as much as an airliner. Everyday he eats about two tons of food. Looking for food is a big job. Most sperm whales are dark gray, but this one is very light-colored, almost white. He is sixty years old.[1]

The whale is swimming about 600 feet (183 meters) below the surface. He pushes himself through the water with his enormous tail. He steers with the fins on each side of his body. Whales are mammals, just like humans. They have lungs, so they have to

SPERM WHALES SURFACE FOR AIR AND DIVE FOR FOOD.

come to the surface for air. This sperm whale is starting to head for the surface when he spots a school of one of his favorite foods: squid.[2] The hungry whale swoops down to attack.

A School of Squid

There are thousands of squid in the huge school. They are eating, too. Squid eat small fish and tiny animals called plankton. Each squid is about three feet long, and the whale can eat hundreds of them at a time. The squid have eight long arms and two tentacles trailing behind their bodies.

Closer and closer the whale comes to the squid. Suddenly, the school speeds up. Have they seen the whale? The whale keeps swimming toward them. Then he senses a big, dark shadow over his head. The shadow comes closer. What could it be? The sperm whale is one of the giants of the ocean. What is this other giant in the sea?

The whale lets the school of squid get away. He rolls onto his side so that he can see what is making the shadow above him. It is an enormous squid. What a meal that will make! The whale turns to chase the big creature.

The Whale Attacks

The giant squid looks much like the small squid the whale usually eats, but this one is almost as long as he is.[3] The whale opens his mouth and tries to bite the squid, but the squid fights back. It quickly has three or four of its

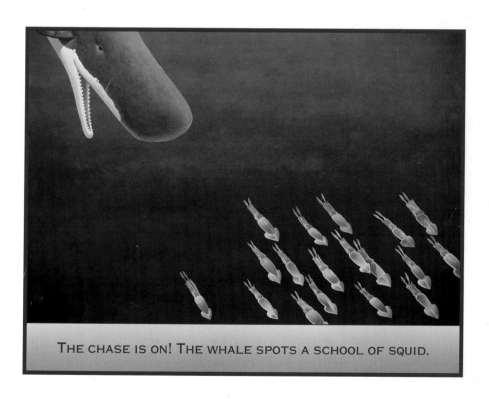

THE CHASE IS ON! THE WHALE SPOTS A SCHOOL OF SQUID.

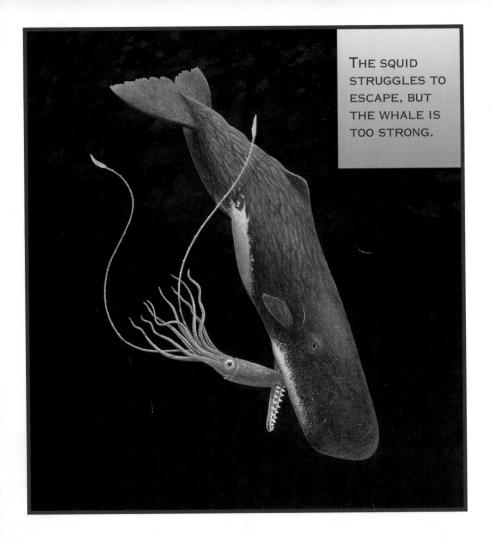

THE SQUID
STRUGGLES TO
ESCAPE, BUT
THE WHALE IS
TOO STRONG.

arms around the whale's head. The squid's powerful suckers dig into the whale's flesh. This is serious.

The whale is running out of air. He must get to the surface and take a breath to continue the fight. With a powerful push of his great tail, he starts up. The squid hangs on. The whale breaks the surface with a huge splash. Still

the squid hangs on. It wraps more arms around the whale's head. The squid is a giant, but the whale is more than one hundred times heavier. The squid fights for its life.

The squid thrashes in the sea beside the whale. The whale slaps its big tail and bursts from the water. The great white whale crashes down on its back. The squid's tentacles are torn from the whale's body. In a burst of strength, the whale turns and bites the squid. The water turns white with foam from the struggling giants. Suddenly, the sea is quiet.

The whale has won the battle. He devours his enemy. His enormous mouth and cone-shaped teeth close on the squid. Then the body of the squid is gone. Some pieces of its arms and tentacles are still floating on the surface. The whale takes a deep breath and dives beneath the waves. The two white flukes of his tail disappear with a splash.

Creatures of Mystery

Some seamen on old sailing ships have said they have seen battles between whales and giant squid. They have said the squid was enormous. It looked like a sea serpent. They called it a beast or a sea monster. They said it was terrifying. No one knows if their stories are true or not.

Giant squid are some of the most mysterious creatures in the sea. Scientists have never seen a giant squid alive, but they know they exist. They have found pieces of giant squid in the stomachs of dead sperm whales. The bodies of dead giant squid have also washed up on beaches. And they have been dragged to the surface in fishing nets.

SINCE NO ONE HAS EVER SEEN A LIVING GIANT SQUID, SCIENTISTS MUST LEARN FROM THE ONES THAT WASH UP ON BEACHES.

But nobody has ever seen a giant squid swimming free in the ocean. No one has ever taken a picture or made a video of a living giant squid. Finding a giant squid alive in the sea is one of the great challenges of ocean exploration.

CHAPTER 2

What *We* *Know* About Giant *Squid*

The giant squid got its name in 1856. By that time, some of them had washed up dead on beaches. Some dead giant squid had been seen by sailors at sea. A science professor in Denmark was fascinated with the reports of these sea monsters. His name was Japetus Steenstrup.

Professor Steenstrup collected stories about giant squid. The earliest story he found was from 1545. That story told about a strange creature found in the sea near Norway. People who saw the animal thought its body looked like the capes and hoods worn by monks, so they called it a sea monk.[1]

FOR CENTURIES, SAILORS TOLD SCARY STORIES ABOUT GIANT SQUID ATTACKING THEIR SHIPS.

The sea monk looked a lot like old drawings of sea monsters. One of the names for these sea monsters was kraken. In the drawings, a kraken was a huge sea beast with arms like snakes. People in Denmark, Norway, and Sweden told scary stories about kraken. Some sailors said their ships were attacked by them.[2]

A New Name

The names *kraken* and *sea monk* lasted for more than three hundred years. By 1856, though, scientists were naming plants and animals according to a new system. Professor Steenstrup renamed the animal *Architeuthis* (ark-i-**tooth**-iss). The name comes from Greek words that mean "chief squid."

These strange animals are huge, but they look a lot like smaller squid. All squid are related to each other in a group of animals called cephalopods (**se**-fall-o-pods), which means "head-foot." That name is a good description. If you look at

THE GIANT SQUID IS RELATED TO THE OCTOPUS, SHOWN HERE.

a squid, you can see that its arms and tentacles come from its head. Octopuses and cuttlefish are relatives of the squid. Cephalopods are a big class of animals.[3]

No Backbones

Squid do not have backbones. Giant squid are the largest animals on Earth without backbones. Their bodies are soft. They have sharp beaks for fighting and eating. All types of squid, including the giant squid, have eight arms, which are about as long as the squid's body. The arms have lots of suckers for grabbing prey.

Squid also have two feeding tentacles, which are much longer than the arms. They have suckers only on the end. The arms and tentacles help the squid hunt and protect itself in the darkness of the deep sea. They can grab food and bring it to the squid's mouth.

Squid come in many colors. They can be red, orange, yellow, black, or brown. Some squid have stripes and spots. Certain

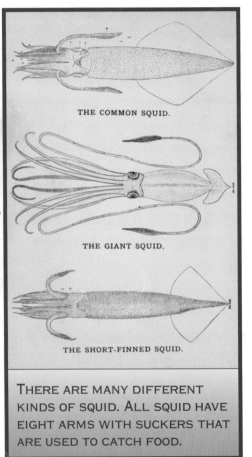

THE COMMON SQUID.

THE GIANT SQUID.

THE SHORT-FINNED SQUID.

THERE ARE MANY DIFFERENT KINDS OF SQUID. ALL SQUID HAVE EIGHT ARMS WITH SUCKERS THAT ARE USED TO CATCH FOOD.

SQUID LOSE THEIR COLOR WHEN THEY DIE. SCIENTISTS CANNOT BE SURE WHAT COLOR GIANT SQUID ARE.

squid can change color to hide when they are frightened or attacked.[4] Since we have only seen dead giant squid, we do not know what color they are when they are alive.

The body of a squid is a tube. Its head is on one end. The tail end is pointed like an arrow. When it swims, the tail end of its body usually goes first, then its head, then the tentacles trail behind. It can also swim headfirst when it is attacking with its arms and tentacles.

Squid take in water and pump it out in a powerful stream from a tube under their heads. The tube is called a funnel. It is muscular and can be turned in any direction. This is how squid can swim either forward or backward.

SMALLER SQUID TRAVEL IN GROUPS, OR SCHOOLS.

Squid can move fast enough to get away from whales and fish that are trying to eat them. Most squid swim in large groups called schools. Giant squid, though, probably swim and hunt alone.

The largest dead giant squid ever found was about 43 feet (13 meters) long, including its arms and tentacles. This great beast came up in the net of fishermen near Norway in October 1939.[5]

The Largest Eyes

The eyes of giant squid are the largest eyes in the animal kingdom. They can be almost 12 inches

(30 centimeters) across. Imagine that! A Frisbee is only 10 inches (25 centimeters) across.

Squid do not blink their eyes. They have no eyelids. Scientists have not been able to get a good look at giant squid eyes. The eyes of dead giant squid are always damaged. The eyes of smaller kinds of squid are probably a lot like the eyes of giant squid, but nobody will know for sure until someone can study a live *Architeuthis*.[6]

THE SQUID'S LARGE EYE HELPS IT TO SEE IN VERY DEEP WATER.

One of the reasons for such large eyes is that the giant squid swims very deep in the ocean. Human eyes can see light only as far down as about 1,600 feet (487 meters).[7] A giant squid can swim much, much deeper than that. Its huge eyes can gather more light than smaller eyes. They let the giant squid see in very deep, dark water. They help it be a great hunter.

What Giant Squid Eat

Giant squid have to eat a huge amount of food every day to grow and stay alive. When a squid is small, it eats small fish, shrimp, and tiny animals called plankton. Bigger squid eat bigger prey.[8]

What does a giant squid eat? Probably larger shrimp, fish, and other squid, but nobody knows for sure. What does a giant squid look like when it is hunting and eating? That is another mystery of the deep. Scientists searching for live giant squid in the wild are trying to solve these mysteries.

CHAPTER 3

Searching *for* Giant Squid

Dr. Clyde Roper is a squid hunter. "I study the giant squid as part of my career-long research on all kinds of squids, octopuses, and cuttlefishes," Dr. Roper said. "They all are really fascinating marine animals . . . but the giant squid is perhaps the most mysterious of all. It is . . . the largest invertebrate [animal without a backbone] ever to live on Earth. I began to study the giant squid many years ago to try to learn the truth . . . about these fascinating, real animals. . . . But there is ever so much more to learn!"[1]

"The single most fascinating thing about the giant squid is that it's never been seen [alive] by anybody,"

said Dr. Roper. Giant squid have washed ashore in Newfoundland, New Zealand, Japan, South Africa, Norway, Iceland, and Denmark. However, no living human being has actually ever seen a healthy giant squid.[2]

"The giant squid is indeed a big animal," Dr. Roper said. "But the trouble with finding it [is that] the ocean . . . covers about two-thirds of the surface of the Earth. On top of that, it is only found in very deep . . . water." Scuba divers cannot dive in very deep water. Only a submarine or robot submarine can dive that deep.[3]

Where to Look for Giant Squid

Dr. Roper knew that sperm whales eat giant squid. He decided to search in a place where there are lots of whales. There might be giant squid around, too. He found a spot in the South Pacific Ocean near New Zealand where there are many sperm whales. It is called Kaikoura Canyon.

Kaikoura Canyon is a trench in the ocean floor. The water is 3,000 to 7,500 feet (914 to 2,300 meters) deep. "The only predator of the giant squid, the sperm whale, stays in the Kaikoura Canyon year-round," said Dr. Roper. There are also many hoki in the area. Hoki are among the giant squid's favorite fish meals.[4]

Dr. Roper also knows that many giant squid have been caught in fishing nets near Kaikoura Canyon. In 1998, eight of the creatures were brought in by fishermen. All were dead. The squid caught in nets were up to thirty feet long, including their tentacles. Parts of much bigger squid have

SOME SCIENTISTS HOPE THAT SPERM WHALES WILL LEAD THEM TO THE GIANT SQUID.

also been found. Dr. Roper and other experts think there are giant squid at least sixty feet (eighteen meters) long.[5]

Expeditions to Kaikoura Canyon

Dr. Clyde Roper and a team of squid hunters traveled to Kaikoura Canyon in 1997. Dr. Roper sent out scouts in small boats to find whales. Bernard Brennan and Gene Feldman were on the whale-searching team. They sped out onto the ocean until they were right over Kaikoura Canyon. Then they lowered special microphones called hydrophones into the sea and waited to hear a whale.

"The boat would slowly drift with the wind and currents," Feldman wrote, "birds would fly by to investigate and one or two even thought that we were interesting enough to land in the water next to us and drift along with the boat. . . . The day wore on."[6]

Finally, Brennan and Feldman heard a whale. Many individual whales can be identified by their sound. Brennan recorded the voice and checked his list of whale names. Its name was Droopy Flukes. The whale's voice sounded like radio static with a hammer hitting something every few seconds.[7]

Brennan and his team recorded lots of whale sounds. They also watched the whales when they came to the surface to breathe. Although they did not see a giant squid during this first research expedition, the researchers learned a lot about the area. They knew it would be a smart place to return to hunt for giant squid.

KAIKOURA CANYON HAS BEEN THE SITE OF SEVERAL SQUID HUNTS OVER THE YEARS.

Return to Kaikoura

In February 1999, Dr. Roper's expedition returned to Kaikoura Canyon on a research ship named *Kaharoa*. Everyone on the team was excited. They hoped to be the first humans to see a living giant squid.

ABOARD THE
RESEARCH SHIP
KAHAROA,
DR. ROPER AND
HIS TEAM OF
SQUID HUNTERS
CONTINUED THEIR
SEARCH FOR THE
GIANT SQUID.

The *Kaharoa* carried a one-person submarine named *Deep Rover*. The squid hunters had cameras and videotape recorders. And they had a lot of questions. How long do giant squid live? What exactly do they eat? How deep do they swim? How quickly do they grow? How big do they really get? How fast are they? Do they live in schools or alone? To answer these and many other questions about giant squid, they first had to find one.

Deep Rover

The squid hunters dived into Kaikoura Canyon in *Deep Rover*. *Deep Rover* looks a little bit like a helicopter. It is about eight feet long, six feet wide, and seven feet high—about the same size as a Volkswagen Beetle. It weighs about three and a half tons when it is out of the water.

Deep Rover can safely dive to a depth of about 3,000 feet (914 meters). It carries one person and enough oxygen for 150 hours underwater. On the dives into Kaikoura Canyon, the sub was connected to the *Kaharoa* by a strong cable

DEEP ROVER IS A ONE-PERSON SUBMARINE THAT TAKES THE SQUID HUNTERS DEEP BELOW THE OCEAN'S SURFACE.

called a tether. (*Deep Rover* can also dive without the tether.) The tether would keep the submarine from drifting too far away. It could also be used to pull the sub back to the surface should the driver lose control.

The pilot drives the sub by controlling thrusters that push it forward, backward, or to the sides. He also controls the sub's four video cameras. The cameras send pictures to the control room on the *Kaharoa*. The sub has bright spotlights. It also has a special sensing device called a sonar. A sonar uses sound waves to tell the pilot what is around the sub even when it is in the dark depths of the ocean.[8]

Into the Depths

On March 10, 1999, everyone on the expedition is excited. The first day of squid hunting with *Deep Rover* has finally arrived. On their last expedition, they did not see a giant squid. Maybe this time they would.

The pilot for this dive is Mike deGruy. Before he descends in *Deep Rover*, he goes over a checklist of 350 items. He makes sure all systems are working. He checks the controls, the cameras, and the safety equipment. The checklist takes more than two hours. Then Mike gives the command to dive.[9]

Deep Rover sinks beneath the surface. On the *Kaharoa*, scientists crowd around the television monitors. Their eyes are glued to the screens. Each scientist has a notebook. They watch the screens and write down the scientific names of the

animals they see. The sub slowly drops to 2,000 feet (610 meters).

They see thousands of small fish, shrimp, and jellyfish. Near the bottom, they see flashing hoki fish. They also see many other kinds of fish. Some are bright silver. Some creatures glow with their own light. This light is called bioluminescence. On the bottom they see yellow and purple starfish and sea urchins.[10]

The first dive ends safely, but Dr. Roper and the squid hunters have seen no whales. And there is no sign of *Architeuthis*.

No Giant Squid, but Lots of Knowledge

For two weeks, *Deep Rover* makes several more dives into Kaikoura Canyon. Dr. Roper and his crew see

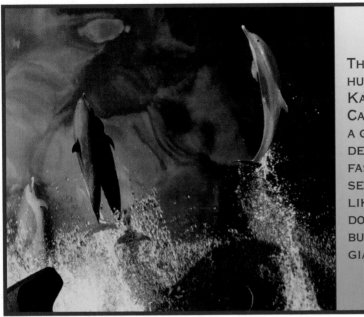

THE SQUID HUNTERS AT KAIKOURA CANYON SAW A GREAT DEAL OF FASCINATING SEA LIFE, LIKE THESE DOLPHINS, BUT NO GIANT SQUID.

many fish, sharks, and dolphins. Then it is time to go home. The scientists are happy with their expedition into the deep sea. They did not see a giant squid, but they have gotten a good look at a place where it lives.

Dr. Roper says he will keep trying. He says he would even take the risk of going down in the submarine to search. "If I thought I could see one of these creatures, I'd go down there on a bicycle," he said.[11]

Though they learned a lot, Dr. Roper and his crew are disappointed that they did not see a living squid.[12] They have searched with submarines, cameras, and modern electronics. Still no human has ever seen a living giant squid.

What other mysteries is the ocean hiding from us? And what mysteries have been solved?

CHAPTER 4

Discovering a *Living* Fossil

The ocean is full of surprises. Although no one has found a living giant squid yet, other mysteries of the deep ocean have been revealed. In 1938, one surprise actually solved an ancient mystery. A biologist named Marjorie Courtenay Latimer was on a dock on the Chalumna River on the southwest coast of Africa. She looked down onto the deck of a fishing boat and saw a strange, bright blue creature she had never seen before.

Latimer was very excited. The captain of the boat said he caught it in his net at a depth of 240 feet (73 meters).[1] He gave the strange fish to Latimer. She took her smelly prize in a taxi to a nearby museum

SCIENTISTS WERE BAFFLED WHEN THIS EXOTIC CREATURE WAS
FOUND NEAR AFRICA.

where she worked. There she measured and studied it closely.
She was very puzzled.

The fish was 54 inches (1.4 meters) long and weighed
127 pounds (58 kilograms). As she worked, its bright blue
color faded to grayish black. The fish had very few teeth in
its big mouth. Its body and fins were covered with large, hard
scales with sharp spines. It had two fins on its back. Most
fish, except sharks, have only one. It had two thick fins near
the head and two on the belly that looked like small legs.[2] Its
tail had three lobes.

Latimer took photographs of the mysterious fish. She
sent a sketch of it to a friend and fish expert named Dr. James
L. B. Smith. He took one look at the sketch and was so
shocked that his wife asked him what was the matter. "This is
from Latimer," Dr. Smith replied. "Don't think me mad, but I

believe there is a good chance that it is a type of fish generally thought to have been extinct for many millions of years."[3]

If Dr. Smith was right, this fish was one of the greatest discoveries in history. He remembered a picture of a fossil fish that looked a lot like Latimer's creature. A fossil is the body of an animal that has turned to rock over millions of years. Many fossils are the only evidence of animals that were once alive but are now extinct.

Dr. Smith dug through his books. There it was! He looked at a drawing of a fossil fish named a coelacanth (**see**-la-canth). Everyone thought the last coelacanths had died at about the same time as the last dinosaurs, 65 million years ago.[4]

To be sure, Dr. Smith went to see Latimer and the fish. It was definitely a coelacanth. This strange creature was a living fossil. Smith named it *Latimeria chalumnae* to honor Latimer and the place where she found it.

Latimer's discovery was front-page news in papers all over the world. The coelacanth was nicknamed Old Fourlegs.[5] A mysterious creature from out of the ancient past had surfaced. The ocean had indeed surprised the world.

What Else Is Hidden Below?

If an animal as big as a giant squid or as secretive as a coelacanth can hide in the sea, what other creatures might be down there? For most of human history, the sea was considered dark, mysterious, and scary. No one knew

MANY TALES HAVE BEEN TOLD ABOUT LIFE IN THE SEA. THE STORIES INVOLVE GIANT SQUID AS WELL AS OTHER MYSTERIOUS OCEAN CREATURES.

what lurked in the depths. People made up stories about sea monsters and weird animals of the ocean.

But the sea is now giving up some of its secrets. Scientists can dive or send equipment into the deepest parts of the ocean. They can observe animals in their natural habitats. They can also study animals they bring up in nets. They carefully report what they see. Mysterious creatures of the sea are continuously being discovered because scientists have the tools and the desire to learn more about the ocean.

Rare Megamouth Shark Discovered

A large filter-feeding shark was first discovered in 1976. This unusual creature shocked scientists. Although many kinds of fish and whales are filter feeders, there are only two other sharks that eat like this. The first megamouth was caught by accident by a Navy research ship that had been dragging two large parachutes in the water.

The Navy delivered the strange beast to Dr. Leighton Taylor, a scientist in Hawaii who studies fish. The shark was 14 feet (4.3 meters) long. It had a huge, soft head and a very large mouth. The inside of its mouth was silvery and the jaws had many small, hooklike teeth. The

THE MEGAMOUTH SHARK WAS FIRST DISCOVERED IN 1976.

unique shark was gray and bluish black, with white on the tips of its fins. It was nothing like any shark ever before seen. Dr. Taylor named it megamouth.[6]

A Real Sea Serpent?

The ocean continues to reveal its secrets, but people sometimes find them just by luck. In 2001, Brian Kakuk and Bill Cooksey were diving near the Bahama Islands. They were inspecting a Navy buoy. Suddenly, a creature five feet long swam up to them. Kakuk and Cooksey were both veteran divers, but neither had ever seen anything like it. The creature looked like a sea serpent.

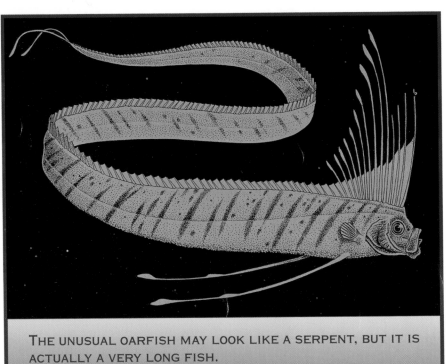

THE UNUSUAL OARFISH MAY LOOK LIKE A SERPENT, BUT IT IS ACTUALLY A VERY LONG FISH.

"It approached and hovered about ten feet away, about twenty feet below the surface. It looked at us . . ." said Cooksey. "Much to my surprise it allowed me to touch the lower part of its body. It was smooth to the touch and fine scaled like a mackerel."[7]

The divers swam to the surface to pick up a video camera. They dived again and recorded pictures of the creature. The strange fish then swam into the depths. Back on shore, Kakuk and Cooksey identified it as an oarfish. They learned that they were the first people to capture one on video.[8]

An oarfish can easily be mistaken for a serpent. But this rare creature is really the longest fish ever found. It can be up to 50 feet (15 meters) long. Its body is very skinny. Oarfish have no teeth. They feed by filtering plankton through their small mouth. Oarfish live at depths of 60–600 feet (18–180 meters). They come to the surface only when injured or dying. It is easy to see how an oarfish thrashing on the ocean surface could look like a sea serpent.[9]

Scary-Looking Creatures

The deep sea hides some very scary creatures that are rarely seen. In 1934, two explorers were the first people to see a living anglerfish. William Beebe and Otis Barton were lowered into the ocean in a steel ball called a bathysphere. No one had ever been as deep as they were going to go.

The deeper they went, the darker the ocean became. About a quarter mile down, it was pitch black. Beebe and

THE ANGLERFISH LIVES IN THE DEEP OCEAN. WILLIAM BEEBE AND OTIS BARTON WERE THE FIRST TO EVER SEE IT.

Barton huddled in the bathysphere. They looked out through two small windows. Down they went into the darkness.

When they were a half mile deep, a frightening creature swam right up to one of their windows. The divers turned on their searchlight. The strange fish had a huge mouth with big fangs. It had a pole that looked like a fishing rod on top of its head. On the tip of the pole was a light.

Beebe and Barton were the first people to see an anglerfish. It lives only in the darkness of the deep sea. An anglerfish uses the light to attract prey such as smaller fish. When the prey approaches, *snap*! It becomes the anglerfish's meal.[10]

Strange Life Around Hydrothermal Vents

In February 1977, three scientists discovered a whole new world beneath the sea. They were diving in a submersible vehicle named *Alvin*, one and a half miles below the surface (about 8,000 feet). They were cruising near a ridge in the seafloor off the coast of South America.

The scientists were studying hydrothermal vents. These are holes in the seafloor. Hot water jets out of the holes. As *Alvin* came close to the vents, the crew saw something very strange. There in the searchlights were colonies of animals living near the hydrothermal vents. The animals were different from any others in the sea. This was almost as wild as finding life on Mars.

"Isn't the deep ocean supposed to be like a desert?" one scientist said to his controller on the surface.

"Yes," replied the controller.

"Well, there's all these animals down here."[11]

Alvin's crew was shocked by what they saw: crabs, shrimp, lobsters, big pink fish, huge clams, and golden brown mussels. Some of these creatures looked almost like their familiar cousins in shallow water. But other creatures

THE SUBMERSIBLE *ALVIN* HAS ALLOWED SCIENTISTS TO DISCOVER ALL SORTS OF NEW AND FASCINATING SEA LIFE.

were nothing at all like anything anybody had ever seen. The strangest of these were wavy things that stood upright off the bottom in long tubes. Reddish tops stuck out at the ends of the tubes. They looked a little bit like giant lipsticks. There were enormous thickets and groves of these creatures all around the vents.

The three people in *Alvin* that day were the first human beings to see most of those creatures. They realized that they

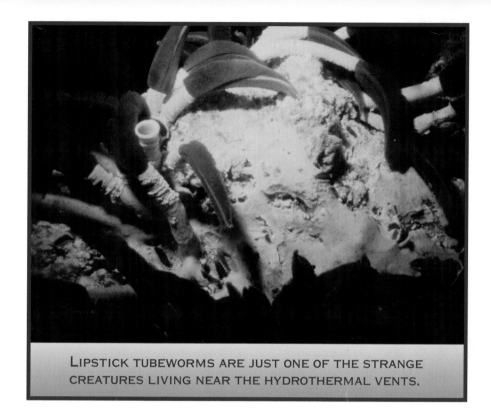

LIPSTICK TUBEWORMS ARE JUST ONE OF THE STRANGE CREATURES LIVING NEAR THE HYDROTHERMAL VENTS.

had discovered an entire new world around the hydrothermal vents. Many more scientists would soon spend a lot of time in *Alvin* trying to figure out what was going on down there.

The water around the first vents they discovered was as warm as the water in a bathtub. The rest of the ocean around them was icy cold. *Alvin*'s crew captured some of the water and took it to the surface. When they opened the sample bottles on the deck of research ship *Lulu*, the scientists smelled rotten eggs. That meant that the water contained a lot of sulfide, a chemical that comes from the inside of the Earth through vents and volcanoes.[12]

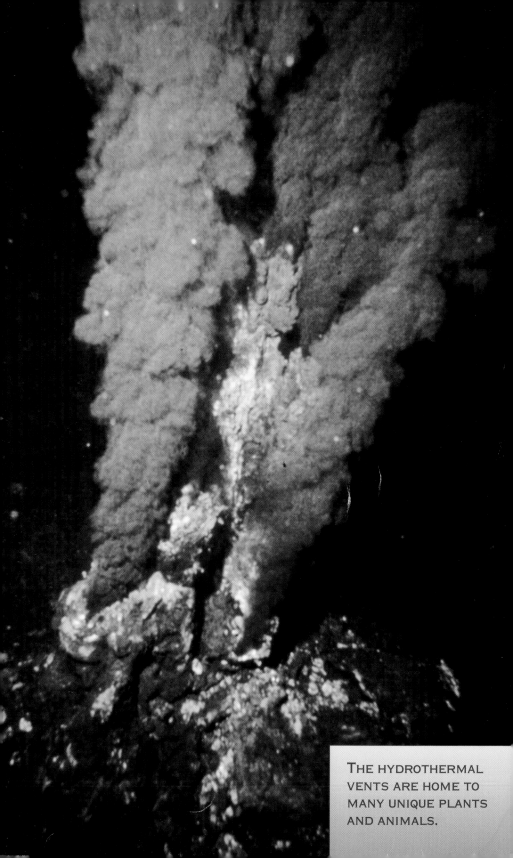

THE HYDROTHERMAL
VENTS ARE HOME TO
MANY UNIQUE PLANTS
AND ANIMALS.

The animals that live around the vents are part of a completely different ecosystem than all others on Earth and the rest of the ocean. An ecosystem is a group of plants, animals, and environmental conditions that depend on one another. The vent ecosystem, unlike all others on Earth, depends on organisms that use the chemical hydrogen sulfide as a source of energy. All other ecosystems depend on the sun and photosynthesis for energy. Ocean explorers had discovered an entirely new way to live in the sea.

Black Smokers

Two years after the first human contact with the creatures of the hydrothermal vents, *Alvin* and its crew discovered another stunning new realm of the abyss. On a dive two miles deep off the coast of Mexico in 1979, the crew saw a giant chimney rising off the bottom of the sea. Inky black smoke was pouring out the top.[13]

The smoking chimney was 65 feet (20 meters) tall. That's about as high as a seven-story building. No one had ever seen anything like it before. Creatures similar to those around hydrothermal vents lived around the black smoker.

Just looking at a black smoker can be frightening. "Raw and powerful, black smokers look like [the totem poles] of an inhospitable planet," said *Alvin* pilot Cindy Lee Van Dover. "I have often worked black smokers in *Alvin* and I never fail to be awed by them."[14]

THE POWERFUL BLACK SMOKERS ARE ONE OF THE MOST AWESOME FEATURES OF THE DEEP SEA.

The Unknown

We have learned a lot about the ocean and its creatures. But the sea still has many secrets. Maybe someday humans will find a giant squid. Maybe we will find entirely new kinds of animals. We know that many creatures remain to be discovered in the depths.

The search continues.

Chapter Notes

Chapter 1. Battle of the Giants

1. Randall R. Reeves, et al, *The National Audubon Society Guide to Marine Mammals of the World* (New York: Alfred A. Knopf, 2002), pp. 240–243.

2. Ibid.

3. Richard Ellis, *The Search for the Giant Squid* (New York: Penguin, 1998), pp. 6–7.

Chapter 2. What We Know About Giant Squid

1. Richard Ellis, *The Search for the Giant Squid* (New York: Penguin, 1998), pp. 60–61.

2. Richard Ellis, *Monsters of the Sea* (New York: Alfred A. Knopf, 1994), pp. 124–125.

3. Ralph Buchsbaum, et al, *Animals Without Backbones,* Third Edition (Chicago: University of Chicago Press, 1987), p. 285.

4. Ellis, *The Search for the Giant Squid*, pp. 43–44.

5. Ibid., p. 261.

6. Ellis, *Monsters of the Sea*, pp. 173–174.

7. William Beebe, "A Roundtrip to Davy Jones's Locker," *National Geographic,* June 1931, p. 655.

8. Ellis, *The Search for the Giant Squid*, pp. 40–41.

Chapter 3. Searching for Giant Squid

1. Discovery Communications, Inc., *Quest for the Giant Squid,* "Ask the Expert Leader," © 2000, <http://dsc.discovery.com/stories/nature/giantsquids/giantsquids.html> (June 22, 2002).

2. Salon.com, *In Search of the Giant Squid* © 2000, <http://www.salon.com/dec96/squid961202.html> (June 22, 2002).

3. Discovery Communications, Inc., *Quest for the Giant Squid,* "Ask the Expert Leader."

4. Ibid.

5. Ibid.

6. Smithsonian Institution, *Search for Giant Squid,* "Dispatches from Kaikoura," © 1999, <http://partners.si.edu/squid/DispatchFrame.html> (July 8, 2002).

7. Ibid.

Chapter Notes

8. Nuytco Research Ltd., "Deep Rover," © 2001, <http://www.nuytco.com/deeprover.html> (July 8, 2002).

9. Smithsonian Institution.

10. Ibid.

11. Salon.com.

12. Smithsonian Institution.

CHAPTER 4. DISCOVERING A LIVING FOSSIL

1. Keith S. Thomson, *Living Fossil: The Story of the Coelacanth* (New York: W.W. Norton & Company, 1991), p. 23.

2. Ibid., p. 24.

3. Ibid., p. 29.

4. Third Wave Media, Inc., *The Fish Out of Time,* "Greatest Fish Story Ever Told: 'Discovery' of the Coelacanth," © 2002, <http://www.dinofish.com> (July 11, 2002).

5. Ibid.

6. Australian Museum, *Find a Fish,* "Megamouth Shark," © 2002, <http://www.amonline.net.au/fishes/fishfacts/fish/megamouth.htm> (October 19, 2002).

7. NAVSEA Newport, "Rare Sighting of Oarfish Filmed," © 2001, <http://www.npt.nuwc.navy.mil/PAO/oarfish.htm> (October 30, 2002).

8. Ibid.

9. J. R. Paxton and W. N. Eschmeyer, eds., *Encyclopedia of Fishes* (San Diego, Calif.: Academic Press, 1995), p. 240.

10. Erich Hoyt, *Creatures of the Deep* (Kingston, Ontario: Firefly Books, 2001), p. 53.

11. William J. Broad, *The Universe Below* (New York: Simon & Schuster, 1997), pp. 105–106.

12. Ibid., p. 107.

13. Ibid., p. 109.

14. Cindy Lee Van Dover, *The Octopus's Garden: Hydrothermal Vents and Other Mysteries of the Deep Sea* (New York: Addison-Wesley Publishing, 1996), p. 101.

Glossary

abyss—Extremely deep ocean.

Architeuthis—The scientific name given to the giant squid. It means "chief squid."

bathysphere—A craft for diving into the deep sea. The word means "deep ball."

bioluminescence—Light produced by a living thing such as a fish or jellyfish.

black smoker—A chimney rising from the floor of the ocean through which hot water and steam pour into the sea.

cephalopod—The group of animals to which squid belong. *Cephalo* means "head" and *pod* means "foot."

cuttlefish—A smaller relative of the giant squid.

ecosystem—A group of plants, animals, and environmental conditions that depend upon one another.

extinct—Vanished from Earth.

flukes—The lobes of the tail of a whale.

fossil—The remains of a plant or animal from the past that usually has turned to rock.

hydrophone—An underwater microphone used to listen for whales and dolphins.

invertebrate—An animal without a backbone.

kraken—One of the names given to giant squid in old stories.

Glossary

mammal—An animal that produces milk for its young, has hair on its body, and breathes with lungs, such as a human, a horse, or a whale.

school—A group of fish, squid, or other swimming animals.

sea monk—A name given to giant squid because their bodies look like the capes and hoods worn by monks.

sonar—An electronic device that uses sound for sensing what is underwater.

tentacles—The two long appendages of squid.

tether—A cable connecting a submarine to its support ship.

Further Reading

BOOKS

Cerullo, Mary M. *The Octopus: Phantom of the Sea*. New York: Cobblehill Books, 1997.

Hoyt, Erich. *Creatures of the Deep: In Search of the Sea's "Monsters" and the World They Live In*. Buffalo, N.Y.: Firefly Books, 2001.

Taylor, Barbara. *The Really Sinister Savage Shark and Other Creatures of the Deep*. New York: DK Publishing, 1997.

Walker, Sally M. *Fossil Fish Found Alive: Discovering the Coelacanth*. Minneapolis, Minn.: Carolrhoda Books, 2002.

INTERNET ADDRESSES

Feldman, Gene Carl. *In Search of Giant Squid*. n.d. <http://seawifs.gsfc.nasa.gov>

PBS Online. *Savage Seas*. "Monsters of the Sea." © 1999. <http://www.pbs.org/wnet/savageseas/deep-side-monsters.html>

Three Wave Media, Inc. *Coelacanth, The Fish Out of Time*. © 2003. <http://www.dinofish.com>

Index